Fire in the Ice Age

Fire in the Ice Age

    Stories of men and women who
    gave priority to the human heart
    and soul and hugged a child
    or loved a stranger.
    Even in the Ice Age.

Sandy McCulloch

Copyright © 2009 by Sandy McCulloch. All rights reserved. No part of this publication may be reproduced, stored in a retrieval system, or transmitted in any form or by any means, electronic, mechanical, photocopying, recording, or otherwise, without the prior written permission of the copyright holder, except brief quotations used in a review.

Design by Meadowlark Publishing Services,
Corvallis, Oregon

ISBN 978-1-61658-302-6
Manufactured in the United States of America.

Published 2009

This book is dedicated to the two people to whom I particularly owe my life as a writer—

Linda Lancione Moyer, of Berkeley, California.

And Natalia Grigor, of Uzhgorod, Ukraine, who committed suicide on 6/9/2006, and for whom I light a candle each Sunday.

Contents

Preface xiii
Acknowledgments xv
Introduction 1
La Casa del Mutilata: a brief case history 3
To Make a Happy Kid 9
The Touch 15
Victor 17
This I Believe: Be in Touch 21
Keep Walking 25
Do You Ever Want to Be Touched? 27
The Good Whore of Palermo 33
Love at the Hotel Enosis 37
The Critical Roles of Touch 41
The Unwanted 45
Attitudes Toward the Gypsy in Southwest Ukraine 51
Alone by the Fire in the Ice Age 53
Beyond Touch 55
The Touched Face 57
Sérife 61
The Farthest Shore: Touch, Evil, and the Forbidden 63
Angel from the North 71
The Price of Experience: a summing up 81
Epilogue 83
Epistle to Be Left in the Earth 85

*The following narrative poem was responsible
for the conception of this book.*

He Sits Down on the Floor of a School for the Retarded

    I sit down on the floor of a school for the retarded,
    A writer of magazine articles accompanying a band
    that was met at the door by a child in a man's body
    who asked them, "Are you the surprise
        they promised us?"

    It's Ryan's Fancy, Dermot on guitar,
    Fergus on banjo, Denis on penny-whistle.
    In the eyes of this audience, they're everybody
    who has ever appeared on TV. I've been telling lies
    to a boy who cried because his favorite detective
    hadn't come with us; I said he has sent his love
    and, no, I didn't think he'd mind if I signed his name
    to a scrap of paper: when the boy took it, he said,
    "Nobody will ever get this away from me,"
    in the voice, more hopeless than defiant,
    of one accustomed to finding that his hiding places
    have been discovered, used to having objects snatched
    out of his hands. Weeks from now I'll send him
    another autograph, this one genuine
    in the sense of having been signed by somebody
    on the same payroll as the star.
    Then I'll feel less ashamed. Now everyone is singing,
    "Old MacDonald had a farm," and I don't know what
        to do

about the young woman (I call her a woman
because she's twenty-five at least, but think of her
as a little girl, she plays that part so well,
having known no other), about the young woman who
sits down beside me and, as if it were the most natural
thing in the world, rests her head on my shoulder.

It's nine o'clock in the morning, not an hour for music.
And, at the best of times, I'm uncomfortable
in situations where I'm ignorant
of the accepted etiquette: it's one thing
to jump a fence, quite another to blunder
into one in the dark. I look around me
for a teacher to whom to smile out my distress.
They're all busy elsewhere. "Hold me," she whispers.
"Hold me."

I put my arm round her. "Hold me tighter."
I do, and she snuggles closer. I half-expect
someone in authority to grab her
or me; I can imagine this being remembered
forever as the time the sex-crazed writer
publicly fondled the poor retarded girl.
"Hold me," she says again. What does it matter
what anybody thinks? I put my other arm around her,
rest my chin in her hair, thinking of children
real children, and of how they say it, "Hold me,"
and of a patient in a geriatric ward
I once heard crying out to his mother, dead
for half a century, "I'm frightened! Hold me!"
and of a boy-soldier screaming it on the beach

x

at Dieppe, of Nelson in Hardy's arms,
of Frieda gripping Lawrence's ankle
until he sailed off in his Ship of Death.

It's what we all want, in the end,
to be held, merely to be held,
to be kissed (not necessarily with the lips,
for every touching is a kind of kiss).

She hugs me now, this retarded woman, and I hug her.
We are brother and sister, father and daughter,
mother and son, husband and wife.
We are lovers. We are two human beings
huddled together for a little while by the fire
in the Ice Age, two hundred thousand years ago.

—Alden Nowlan

Preface

A few days before Christmas of 2008 I was given a collection of poetry that included the narrative poem you have just read. I was not familiar with Nowlan, but I was greatly affected by this poem. I showed it to friends and found that their reactions fell into two quite different clusters. The majority thought it a poem about retarded children—probably Down syndrome children. But others responded in a completely different fashion, reading it as a statement regarding the enormous importance of being touched, held, *physically held and touched and loved as children*. This book is about physical love and what it means to a child. Indeed, what it means even to human survival. In an Ice Age.

Time that is intolerant
Of the brave and innocent,
And indifferent in a week
To a beautiful physique,

Worships language and forgives
Everyone by whom it lives;
Pardons cowardice, conceit,
Lays its honours at their feet.
—W. H. Auden

Acknowledgments

I am greatly indebted to the following men and women who have most notably shaped the making of this book. *Reverends Timothy Stover and Jeff Hale,* who contributed valuable chapters. *Linda Lancione Moyer,* who caused me to become a writer. The late *Natalia Grigor McCulloch,* of Ukraine. The modern Turkish miniaturist known as *Hassan,* who drew the figures on the back cover. *Bill Shumway,* Corvallis artist *par excellence,* who painted the main image for the front cover. And finally, my truly first-rate editor, *Sheridan McCarthy.* I have had several quite good editors during my time as a writer, and Sheridan stands above them all.

I could not possibly thank all of you enough.

I set myself the task of writing of people as they are.
A man sets himself the task …

A man sets himself the task of drawing the world. As the years pass, he fills the empty spaces with images of provinces and kingdoms, mountains, bays, ships, islands, fish, houses, instruments, stars, horses, and people. Just before he dies, he discovers that the patient labyrinth of lines traces the image of his own face.
—Jorge Luis Borges

Introduction

Over the past few hundred years, British and American cultures have been relatively touch-phobic. Physical intimacy—public and private—has been frowned upon in many ways and in many different aspects of our lives. Since the 1960s, attitudes have changed to some degree in the United States, but far more change is needed if we are to resemble most of the world's societies.

The following collection of stories will attempt to describe many different aspects of the importance of human touch and human physical contact. For the purpose of this introduction, I shall mention just one of them, a story that to me represents the black hole of sensory deprivation. The Ice Age *in extremis*, if you will.

In the earliest years of the twentieth century in the United States, a single woman of the middle or upper class would be socially ruined by an accidental pregnancy. Often her solution was to travel a few hundred miles away from her home, deliver her baby, and then leave it immediately in an orphanage or foster home. The foster homes provided for such occasions were typically able to bottle-feed the newborn children and change their diapers a few times a day but lacked the funds and personnel to do much more. The orphaned newborns simply lay on their backs in rows of cribs, and *were rarely picked up, touched, fondled, or otherwise given human contact.* As a result of this deprivation, it is a published fact that in some foster homes the mortality rates within the first year of life ranged from 20 percent to as high as 60 percent. If one is not touched, one may die.

It is as simple as that. *If one is not picked up and held and touched, one may die.*

La Casa del Mutilata: a brief case history

The greater part of this book will consist of personal histories and stories about men and women who manifest—in various ways—the effects of touch, physical contact, and human warmth. Or the lack of such human contact. Therefore it seems only appropriate that we begin with stories of the author.

I was born in 1930, after three decades during which Americans had been told by most respected authorities, "You should not hold your child, and do not pick him up when he cries," and so forth. And breast-feeding of infants was not considered appropriate for much of the middle and upper classes.

My first decade is difficult for me to recall with accuracy, but I am told that my mother attempted to breast-feed me for three weeks before someone demonstrated minimal brains and weighed me. It seems that I had nearly died of starvation.

One day before I was two I was allowed to wander into the kitchen, reach up to the stove, and pull a pot of boiling water down on myself. I was unconscious in a hospital for five days afterward and was not expected to live. Also during my first ten years (and until the age of eighteen), I sucked my thumb obsessively, relentlessly, against determined, elaborate, and frantic efforts to make me stop.

I can remember being scolded during my teen years for holding a girl's hand in public. Until I finished high school—barely graduating—I was by any reasonable standard a social and academic basket case.

Somehow, upon entering college I turned most of this around. I did reasonably well socially and graduated with honors. Then, between the ages of twenty-two and thirty-nine, I accomplished the following:

- an MS in zoology from UCLA
- a successful career teaching science in two San Francisco area colleges
- three marriages and three divorces

There is a well-known phrase in baseball: three strikes, you're out. As far as I could tell, my third marriage was, finally, a success. I adored Margaret and firmly believed that our marriage would last forever. Months after she left, however, she told me she had done so *because she could not tell whether I had loved her or not.*

Until the age of thirty-nine, the simple fact is that I had been a walking emotional dead man, almost entirely lacking in affect.

Affect:
A. to touch the emotions of …
B. feelings or emotions, especially as expressed physically
C. to influence [through emotions]

I was then, and am now, an intelligent man. But approaching middle age and with three failed marriages behind me, I finally became aware of the pitiful fact that something was quite wrong with me. I could remember, looking back in pain, that there'd been warning signs. Now I was certain. I had no idea on earth what was wrong, or what to do about it; I only knew that I had a lot of work ahead. All I could do was begin a search. And so I began … Looking back, I was a blind man stumbling in the dark. But I began …

Between 1969 and 1974 I did five years of very hard psychological work on myself. This involved various kinds of psychotherapy, but primarily the then popular psychological awareness groups, which were also known as encounter growth groups or human potential groups. Initially I had no idea what I was trying to do, but in 1969 I stumbled into these groups and found that I loved them for their intensity. (Many other people were threatened by such intensity, and ran from them.)

Many of these workshops involved forceful verbal exploration, sexual questions, much touching and physical contact, nudity, and occasionally, actual sexual acts.

As I said, I loved the intensity, which offered the healing that my dead soul needed, and I ended up running a series of these groups between 1971 and 1980 in my Berkeley home, working with as many as fifty people a week. These were advertised as "divorce support groups." Divorce was, after all, the one area in which I was an expert! (Teach what you know best …)

Between 1965 and 1974, the counterculture years, there was a popular book titled *Please Touch!* The healing of the previous touch-starved decades was a main point, and a great deal of touching went on.

I am going to say very little more about my personal involvement in these growth groups. I find it quite painful to think about much of this time even thirty-five years later. But I can look back on those five years of work and single out one extremely revealing high point. I shall share this with you and then move on to others' stories.

In perhaps 1973 I was at a weekend workshop (Friday

night to Sunday noon) at the Esalen Institute in Big Sur with a nationally known Gestalt therapist, Stella Resnick. In Gestalt groups it was customary for one person at a time to work on what was generally called the "hot seat." (Stella called hers the "love seat," and in her groups at Esalen it was a big soft pillow.)

The Resnick group, like many others of that period, involved perhaps twenty people seated on soft pillows in a circle. The floor was covered with a thick, soft rug. Several people had worked in the opening Friday night session. I recall the Saturday morning session as warm and relaxed, with sunlight pouring through the open sliding-glass doors.

Stella asked, "All right, who wants to work?" Everyone was happy, lying back on their pillows. No one volunteered.

"Okay. Nobody wants to work?" Stella said. "Then I will take care of myself and satisfy my curiosity." She pointed to one and then another person and simply asked briefly, "Tell me about yourself."

Then she looked at me and said, "Who are you? Tell me about your father." It was to be one of the peak moments of my life, perhaps the Everest … and I had absolutely no idea what was about to happen. I was a lamb being led to the slaughter by a world expert.

"My father made me what I am, for better and worse. He was a hateful man. I am the product of my father."

"Tell me about your mother," said Resnick.

"My mother had nothing to do with me. She was a nonentity. I was made what I am by my father, entirely him."

And Resnick said, *"Really!"*

Bear in mind, Gestalt therapy teaches that one must pay a great deal of attention to the largely unconscious activities of the body; body signals count greatly at times.

"Look at your feet," she told me. I looked down to find my toes wagging furiously up and down.

Resnick threw the big soft "love seat" pillow out into the middle of the circle and said, "There's your mother! Stand on her and talk to her!"

I innocently stood up, walked over and stood on the pillow, looked down, looked up at the sky, down again, and then for a few minutes I simply went mad. I stood on that pillow and simply shrieked at the sky. I screamed over and over,

Touch me!
Touch me!
For God's sake, touch me,
Touch me-e-e-e …
Touch me-e-e-e …

I screamed for what seemed like two or three minutes, and then stood there on that pillow and sobbed for a few more minutes. Finally I staggered off the pillow and started to walk toward the door to the bathroom. A quiet, soft voice behind me said,

"Please don't go."

It was Resnick, and I remember that voice—thirty-five years later—as the most loving sound I have ever heard in all my years.

Fire in the Ice Age, indeed …

To Make a Happy Kid

Since I opened this book with a worst-case scenario, let me now give you what I consider the *best* case I have encountered in my seventy-eight years.

During the 1980s I built and ran a retreat—a collection of small rental cabins—in a redwood forest near Mendocino, California. A woman reserved a cabin for herself, for a three- or four-day stay, as I recall. She arrived late one afternoon with a two-year-old child in her arms, and my immediate reaction was that the baby was one of the happiest-looking kids I'd ever seen in my life. I complimented Mom, and her response was (I'm quoting her exactly):

"I have breast-fed her on demand for two years, and am now just about ready to wean her."

One month later I was in the Mendocino town laundromat when an acquaintance, the wife of the local doctor, came in. With her came her four-year-old son. Smiling and bouncing happily, with an air of "The world is my oyster!", the kid jumped into a chair and began reading a small book. He glowed with satisfaction.

I happened to know this mother well enough to ask a personal question. So, thinking of the earlier encounter, I asked her.

"Tell me, did you breast-feed your lovely son?" Her exact response:

"I breast-fed him on demand until he was *four years old*, and just weaned him a few weeks ago."

The British writer Bruce Chatwin wrote a lovely collection of travel stories, *What Am I Doing Here?*, that included a wonderful chapter of observations on nomad cultures. Titled "Nomad Invasions," it offered the following choice passages. The references apply primarily to the classic Central Asian horseback-riding, nomad tribes.

> A primary need for movement is borne out by recent studies of human evolution. Professor John Napier has shown that the long-striding walk is an adaptation, unique among the primates, for covering distances over open savannahs. The bipedal walk made possible the development of the manufactory hand, and this led to the enlarged brain of our species. Any human baby also demonstrates its instinctive appetite for movement. Babies often scream for the simple reason they cannot bear to lie still. *A crying child is a very rare sight on a nomad caravan* [emphasis mine], and the tenacity with which nomads cling to their way of life, as well as their quick-witted alertness, reflects the satisfaction to be found in perpetual movement. As settlers, we walk off our frustrations. The medieval Church instituted pilgrimage *on foot* as a cure for homicidal spleen. ... We should perhaps allow human nature an appetitive drive for movement in the widest sense. The act of journeying contributes towards a sense of physical and mental well-being, while the monotony of prolonged settlement or regular work weaves patterns in the brain that engender fatigue and a sense of personal inadequacy.
>
> *On long journeys:* Without milk from domesticated animals and without beasts of burden, the

mothers must suckle *and* carry their children on long journeys at the age of three or more. Meanwhile, they cannot bear any more children.

At encampment: As economic principle, nomads make no effort to limit births, and a plentiful supply of milk from domesticated animals enables a nomad mother to conceive again immediately after birth. Her first child is weaned early and to some extent this rupture weakens the bond of attachment between her and her infant. The latter deflects its attachment onto animal "substitutes" and is encouraged to fondle baby animals, remaining "animal-fixed" for life.

To summarize, these are Chatwin's descriptions of the horseback-riding, cattle-herding nomads of Central Asia. People we know historically as the Mongols and Turks. A people always on the move. When traveling, the mothers usually carry a baby in a sling across their breasts. (On long distances, until the age of three, according to Chatwin.) Older children are commonly carried in slings across the back, with the kids peering bright-eyed over Mother's shoulders. *Always on the move. Kids always in contact with their mothers. And Chatwin remarks that these children almost never cry.* (Why would they?! Always movement, contact with the mother, rich visual stimulation. And breast-fed, often until the age of three …)

It is said that in Asia some portion of nomad culture still survives. (I would bet a fair sum that some now carry cell phones.) By a lovely chance, a few years ago in a vast plaza in front of the Beyazit Mosque in *European* Istanbul, here came two Turkic Asian nomad women! I began photographing them from a distance. *They looked like photographs straight out of a* National Geographic! I could hardly believe my eyes! Handsome robes and scarves. One had a baby in a breast sling, and both women had small older children (three or four years old) in back slings, peering over their shoulders.

I had hoped the two nomads would not notice my camera, but they had good eyes. When they saw me, they slowed down, then walked up to me in curiosity. We shared no common language, and I am quite stupid in other tongues, having never traveled abroad until I was fifty-three. Since the nomads and myself could not speak to one another, we soon separated. But I kept the photos in my files, and one of them ends this chapter.

I cannot resist a final remark that *may* be irrelevant, or perhaps not. If the mother's pleasure matters at all, please be advised that during breast-feeding some women experience orgasm, over and over and over. I once was close for several years to a lovely woman who hailed from a large city in central California. She had had only one child (had wanted ten!) and had breast-fed him until his teeth came in and breast-feeding became quite painful. The point? During the act she had had orgasm after orgasm. She was so happy with this that *after* weaning her son she had advertised herself widely as an expert babysitter for kids in the first months of life! Joyful mothers trapped at home with a newborn could take a break and go to a movie! And my friend's milk would not dry up! Barbara nursed many babies and had many, many orgasms, the parents were blissfully ignorant, and a good time was had by all. True story!

Pravda.

Turkic nomads in Istanbul. Photograph by the author.

The Touch

Sometime back in the 1970s a young man and a young woman were headed over the mountains toward the Mendocino coast of California. She was hitchhiking. He was driving a pickup, and he gave her a ride. There was an old country store at the halfway point, and he stopped to buy a six-pack of beer. Later he told her that when he bought the beer, and she stayed with him, he thought she was giving him "permission" for what came next.

A short time later, down the road, he pulled the truck over, took the girl firmly by the arm, and marched her into the woods. He ordered her to take off her skirt and lie down. He removed his lower clothes and lay down on top of her, and prepared to enter her body.

The girl reported later to her friends that she looked up at him and his face seemed desperate, tortured, agonized. She reached up and gently stroked one hand down the side of his face. The man collapsed sobbing. Then arose apologizing profusely, handed her her clothes, took her back to his truck, and delivered her to her destination in Fort Bragg on the coast.

Only one touch. One tender stroke down the side of a tortured face …

Victor

Victor was a man I met a number of times while I lived in Ukraine between 2001 and the year he died, 2003. He was a good friend of my wife, Natalia. I was told he would take $1,000 cash to kill a man. I was led to believe that he would perform this service for Natalia without cost …

The following somewhat abbreviated account begins after we met Victor on the street one afternoon and he dragged the two of us to a nearby café …

Victor was a Soviet fighter pilot in Afghanistan for two years. He saw so much horror, so much evil, perhaps he participated in so much, that in the end it destroyed him. The once superb human being was being eaten alive by the pain of Afghanistan, and the only readily available painkiller was vodka. I watched his face as he talked to Natalia. Alcohol is, in technical terms, a de-inhibitor. One drinks, and whatever is inside roars out. Happy? One is then a happy drunk. This man, however, was filled with rage; his bullet head and face were beaded with sweat, and his eyes were loaded with pain and menace. No one at this moment would have crossed him. When he ordered the café owner to change the music, or raise the volume, he was instantly obeyed. No sane man would have refused.

Over the next several months, I occasionally saw him on the streets. He appeared not to recognize me. I would imagine him flying fighter planes, and thought of him as a man to be feared. He drank a good bit of vodka, and certainly, by reputation, was a man who could kill in seconds. But then one morning Natalia and I met Victor on the street and found a completely broken soul. He walked up to us so quietly that he could have been a shadow or a ghost, and he begged her for a few kopek—pennies—to buy a shot of vodka. He had fallen off the edge of the world and was humbly begging for vodka. Natalia later told me this happened once or twice a year, for a week or so at a time.

Natalia would not give him money on the street. We went to a nearby workers' café in the market, and she bought each of us a small shot of vodka. Victor sat across a long table from us, and we each knocked down the shot. Then, for some reason, Natalia left the table and walked back to the bar: Victor and I were alone. I looked across the table at this half-mad and much feared man and saw that all that was left was a broken shell. He was slumped against the table. We looked into each other's eyes—and his eyes had changed. They were no longer the eyes of a savage; they held no challenge or pride. The man was broken. And then I saw what indeed was in those eyes. He was open, he was available, *he was sitting on the edge of his open grave, and he knew it. All that was left was need. But for what?*

I reached my hand across the table. He took it in his and then covered it with his other hand. I did the same. We held each other's hands; we looked into each other's eyes and held each other, and for a few moments we were as little children.

You do understand that we shared no language.

You do understand, this was irrelevant.

You do understand, if I was in some way a small gift to the man, then equally, he was a gift for me.

You do understand? Listen! And you will hear nothing!

DO you understand? Between a man and a baby or a small child, words are useless. Between a man and a horse, there are no words. In our Uzhgorod neighborhood there are guard dogs, trained to be vicious, that a man approaches only at his peril. But *my dear wife simply puts her arms around them. Between a woman and a dog, there are no words. And between Victor and myself was no common language. When Victor possessed words, he was a rage-filled, half-destroyed man who could kill in an instant. When words abandoned him, we were as little children.*

Look, words are mostly for lying. Words come from the mind, but only rarely from the human heart. Maugham said it all. Words *"… can only tell you that the umbrella of the gardener's aunt is in the house."* Occasionally, however, there can be an exception.

Anna Swir, poet of Poland, has taken the essence of what is human and, in a rare treasure, put it into words. Rarely, only very rarely, words seem to do justice to the human heart and soul. Here are her words.

> *Walking to your place for a love feast*
> *I saw at a street corner*
> *an old beggar woman.*
>
> *I took her hand*
> *kissed her delicate cheek,*
> *we talked, she was*
> *the same inside as I am,*
> *from the same kind,*
> *I sensed this instantly*
> *as a dog knows by scent*
> *another dog.*
>
> *I gave her money,*
> *I could not part from her.*
> *After all, one needs*
> *Someone who is close.*

And then I no longer knew
why I was walking to your place.

On Orthodox Easter Sunday of 2003 I learned that Victor had been murdered. *Rest in peace, Victor.* It no longer matters that the umbrella of the gardener's aunt is in the house.

This I Believe: Be in Touch
Rev. Timothy Stover

Most mornings, my day begins with an opportunity to provide basic, essential nurturing and care for another being. It happens as first my dog Shasta and then my cat Dakota present themselves to me for their morning massage. Free of any hint of embarrassment or shame, they make themselves available for this gift of touch and, just as freely, express their great appreciation and satisfaction in receiving it. Just as it is clearly of benefit for them to receive, so is it beneficial for me to give.

And this I believe: we all might benefit greatly from understanding, accepting, even affirming what Shasta and Dakota seem to get so clearly—that the gift of touch, both in giving and receiving, is elemental to our emotional, physical, and spiritual well-being. It is a gift we should share generously and with great caring.

It is, of course, ironic that this power of touch should be so readily embraced by these animals, precious as they are. But it's also the irony of our life in higher education: as we study and nurture our intellect, growing in our propriety and professionalism in accord with the nature of the institutions in which we seek to serve, we increasingly come to distrust and/or devalue the emotional and physical parts of ourselves and others.

We have come to a time and place where we are literally out of touch with one another, and yet our basic need for touch doesn't diminish. We push it aside at our peril. Being out of touch may be what is at the root of many of the addictions in our culture—addictions that arise as we hunger for authentic touch and yet try to satisfy that hunger with unfulfilling substitutes.

Being out of touch may cause us to supplant healthy sensuality with unhealthy sexuality and find ourselves enmeshed in relationships that neither satisfy nor serve either person in them.

This distortion of our need for touch may even cause us to conclude that harsh touch is better than no touch, so we find ourselves accepting violence upon ourselves and perpetrating it on others.

A truly "higher education" should be one that honors the whole person as he or she is engaged fully in the education enterprise. Learning to let touch back into our shared living can be a powerful and healing experience.

Two of the most important elements in my own professional development had to do with giving myself over to the power of touch. The first came as I entered the final year of my seminary training. Once a week for twelve weeks I found a new and profound sense of vulnerability and trust as I literally placed myself in the hands of a bodywork specialist. Together we found ways for me to move more freely and live more fully in the world.

The second came as I was in transition between ministry settings and healing following a divorce. In an attempt to more fully understand my more informal experiences with massage, I spent nine months training for licensing as a massage therapist. This period challenged some of my old understanding and assumptions about the human body and taught me to live with new ones. More importantly, it was a time of trying to better understand and trust what people meant when they told me I had "healing hands." I came to understand, and I truly believe, that we all have healing hands when we offer the gift of touch with the clear intention of caring for and nurturing others. I also believe that the gift comes back: as we touch, so we are touched in return.

Let's be in touch.

Timothy Stover
January 15, 2007

Keep Walking

> Any human baby also demonstrates its instinctive appetite for movement. Babies often scream for the simple reason they cannot bear to lie still. A crying child is a very rare sight on a nomad caravan.
> —Bruce Chatwin

The very earliest memory I can recall from my entire life is of a cold street corner in Lancaster, Pennsylvania. I was probably between two and three years old. Easily able to walk about, but in certain matters, quite spoiled.

My mother was pushing me in a stroller. She was stopped on a street corner by three old busybody women. They were scolding her!

"Elizabeth, he's much too old to be pushed in a stroller! He's almost grown up! Take him out of the stroller. Make him walk! Make him walk!"

When I realized what the old women were saying, I began shrieking at the top of my lungs! Drowned them out! My mother, unable to hear anything and obedient to the prevailing reality, soon pushed me on down the street. Damn right, I screamed: if you won't hold me, at least push me…!

Do You Ever Want to Be Touched?

This story describes a small part of a remarkable and sometimes surreal relationship that took shape in Oregon near the end of the twentieth century. Names, dates, and places are fictional. The reality is pretty much as you read it.

Elizabeth and I shared three sharply defined periods in time: *Doctor/patient*, *Friends*, and *Lovers*. The boundaries between each were quite sharp and entirely controlled by Elizabeth. The story here describes the quite real and nonfictional jump from "Friend" to Lover. And it begins with a brief description of what it meant for us to be friends.

Over a period of twelve months, from one June to another, Elizabeth Vaccari and I became friends. We enjoyed one another very much. However, this friendship was unlike any usual human connection. A pattern developed and soon became a fixed and rather precise ritual: Friday evening dinner in a public place or, once or twice, a lunch.

We shared a mutually enjoyable meal in a restaurant — once a month.

The time and place were largely as she chose.

We never touched. As I recall it, we never even shook hands. Certainly we never kissed each other; the erotic was light-years removed.

She never spoke of introducing her children or inviting me to her home. I had a beautiful home on the rural west edge of town, but I never dreamed of inviting her there. The assumption was firmly in place: this is an impersonal friendship to be carried out in public places.

I vividly recall that our parting ritual was always abrupt and initiated by her.

We would spend anywhere from two to four hours in happy conversation. Sometimes this dealt with personal matters, but more often it was about her medical practice or my Mediterranean travels. Elizabeth spoke wistfully, sometimes eagerly, even during the first summer, of making a first trip to Europe. "You will take me to Venice in the fall of next year." (Not bloody likely, I thought.) And then, suddenly — once, I remember, after a quite brief dinner — her voice would change. Elizabeth had gone away and Dr. Vaccari's quiet but stern voice would announce, "*I am going to go now.*" No mutual exchange of parting thoughts. Little if any social grace. It was as if a sweet and lovely woman, enjoying an evening out, were suddenly to vanish and be replaced by a golem. And the golem fled.

Then after a full year of these enjoyable but impersonal restaurant meetings, there came a strange moment. It must have been in early June 1975. We had shared a lunch. I remember that it was a lovely sunny day, and the city park was full of flowers. Elizabeth got into her car. I stood beside the door, and she rolled down the window to allow a last word. I bent down toward her — and I suddenly had the strongest urge to reach into the car with my left hand and stroke it gently down the right side of her upturned face. I did not. I think she would have ripped it off. But the thought hung in my mind like a sweet flower. I could not tell whether the flower was in truth a bud about to open or was to be a stillborn freak. But the thought hung there in my skull, it hung there, and a day or so later I sent Elizabeth a brief note. The last line was a simple question.

"Do you ever want to be touched?" And something changed.

During the following days I received two brief notes from Elizabeth. The first may have been mailed before she received the question, "Do you ever want to be touched?" But the second note was clearly an answer to my question.

> 6/28
> I can come to your home on July 4. I can be there one-ish. Will this work for you?
> Elizabeth

It was a seismic rearrangement of ritual!

On July 4, 1975, Elizabeth Vaccari came to my home. She spent several hours sitting in my sunshine-filled backyard and lying in the hammock hung between the branches of a huge oak. We visited. We had our first hours of tentative personal exploration. We *truly* talked. And all at once our previous four years of ordinary reality were shattered upon the ground.

Because I have lived alone most of my life, not by choice but by karma, I have known *en passant* a number of remarkable and extraordinary men and women. To be single is to be free to touch the *Wandervogel,* as well as to touch loneliness. The extraordinary, the strong, the angry, the frightened—such souls sometimes approach one another in strange ways. They do not always ask for dates and kiss on the third evening; they are not always polite or inclined to explain. They simply break upon one another. This is what Elizabeth chose to do: she gave orders. Her voice was quiet. It was devoid of any obvious emotion, devoid of doubt or passion or audible need. The voice was simply stern. But it was a voice that few sensible men on earth would have disobeyed.

"Come in the bedroom.

"Stand here, in front of me.

"Do not talk. Just listen."

Then, standing a foot in front of me, her eyes looking up eight or nine inches into mine, Elizabeth—this tiny woman whom I did not really know at all—said,

"I am going to take off my dress. I want you to look at me. Do not touch me, and do not say anything." She unbuttoned the top few buttons of her light summer dress and shrugged her shoulders, and the fabric fell in a limp, small pile around her feet. She wore nothing else. I shall remember that moment all my life—it is all etched in my brain. The woman was perhaps fifty years old; she was gaunt, emaciated, skeletal, all bone, skin, and small slender muscles. And at that moment she was the bravest and most beautiful woman I had ever seen in my life. We simply stood there for seconds. The clock never moved; I am sure that it stood still. And then, at intervals, she gave more instructions:

"I want you to run your hands over my shoulders and down my back. Stroke me. But do not speak.

"Now hold my buttocks. Stroke them.

"Now hold your hands on my breasts.

"Now you may run your hands over my legs. Do not speak.

"Now you may touch me anywhere you want …"

Elizabeth repeatedly said I should not speak. It was a nearly irrelevant order; I was quite speechless, in shock. For two minutes or more, her instructions continued and I gently obeyed. And then a long silence fell between us. She looked into my eyes. I looked into hers. It seems in hindsight that she had run out of orders and simply did not know what to do next. Then, to my utter surprise, leaving her dress on the floor, she started to walk out of the room! As she walked by my bed, I finally found my own voice—

"Get in the bed!"

It was as if an invisible hand had grasped the tiny body and simply flung it through the air. She rose into the air, leapt beneath the quilt, and disappeared. All that remained of the visible Elizabeth was a small patch of dark curly hair at the top of the bed. And a tiny, motionless outline in the bedding, a small tracing of a figure that might have been a frightened ten-year-old girl. But that is not what it was …

Much later that evening Elizabeth went home.

During the next few weeks, I received several letters from Elizabeth. Two of them are particularly choice, so I will share them here. *These are not fiction.*

> 7/6
>
> Baker—
>
> I am fifty years old and I have never ever ever before received a dozen roses. It is even possible I have never before received flowers from a man. At least I cannot recall.
>
> It has been a long long time since I have had the opportunity to experience the sensations that are evoked by the phrase
> "To take your breath away"… ah

> 7/19
>
> Baker—
> I will be at your home Saturday evening; if you will cook dinner for me and you will take the medication and you will have a bed made up with fresh linen.
> E–

Without going into details, our love relationship lasted for many months. It finally ended very badly after a period during which Elizabeth became quite ill and endured periods of severe psychotic depression.

Be careful of those things you deny. Aldous Huxley once said, "Pain is an opinion." Certainly that is *his opinion*. However, it is a real opinion deeply built into ancient parts of the human brain. I do not pretend to be better than my brain …

When I was a child in North Carolina we had glass ceiling fixtures in our house that were like concave dishes facing up. In the summer they filled up with bugs. After a while there would be a scatter of dead bodies. Then a collection large enough to be obvious. Then a puddle of dead bugs large enough to block some light. Usually we would wait until the bulb burned out. Then we would clean the glass and dump the bugs. Then it would start over. After I grew up I became like the bugs. Drawn to the light and warmth, I warm myself by being close to a beloved woman. And then, like the bugs, I die.

But I die over and over.

The Good Whore of Palermo

A reader's eye is often captured by a title such as this. I have known otherwise respectable middle-aged women who, when visiting a bookstore, would abruptly stop in their tracks to peruse a book with a title such as *The Brothels of Bangkok*. And therefore you are forewarned: this is a dull story. It is a story, in fact, in which nothing bad happens at all. Of badness there is only a faint whiff on the evening breeze.

Not far from La Vucciria market in Palermo there is a large piazza that consists entirely of a rectangle of concrete surrounded by a number of banks and a rooftop machine gun nest. This is a banking square, and this is a Mafia neighborhood. During daylight hours on weekdays, the piazza is covered with parked automobiles, pedestrians, perhaps twenty policemen, and a soldier in a sentry box carrying an automatic weapon. At night, of all of this, only the solitary sentry remains; most of the good citizens of Palermo have locked themselves into their houses. My hotel overlooked this square. The man at the hotel desk was a rigid and frightened old Cattolico with the eyes of a hanging judge and a bitter steel-trap mouth. His mouth said, "Be back to the hotel by midnight. Then we lock the door." His eyes said, *Don't go out after dark at all.* At night the piazza was a place for whores.

One rather subdued young woman was a regular fixture at the corner just opposite my third-floor window, but six or seven others often came by and idled there. Often, these girls laughed and joked with the carloads of young men who drove by to look them over. Often, a car would circle the block, and the women would laugh and wave and kick out their beautiful, long legs. The car would circle the block again, perhaps, and one of the girls would briefly pop up her blouse, with a peal of laughter, to expose her ample breasts. The banter was generally around issues of the flesh and manhood. "You boys are just making noise, you are children. You can't afford us. And if you had the lire, you wouldn't know what to do, si? So boring."

And then one night, an old tiny red Fiat stopped to chat—and the engine died. The Fiat would not go ...

Two girls happened to be at the corner. Instantly, they jumped behind the Fiat and pushed furiously; the little car rolled away briskly, the engine caught and roared, and the little red Fiat disappeared around a corner and out of sight. To me this seemed a bit odd. Surely the Fiat carried potential customers; who else would be abroad in the Mafia precincts of Palermo after nightfall? The girls were helping their customers leave? But wait! Here came the little red Fiat around the block and up to the curb again. And again, when it stopped the engine died. One of the two girls had left. The other immediately stepped behind the little car again and, her long bare legs working madly, pushed it slowly ten feet or so. Where it rolled to a stop, going nowhere.

Just then a motor scooter roared around the corner. With an air of complete confidence, the young prostitute stepped into the street. Planting her legs well apart, she held up an imperious, high right arm and hand. STOP, said her body; she was as confident as any policeman in Sicily, and the men screeched to a halt. She pointed at the Fiat and commanded the two young men. They leaped behind the car; instantly it started rolling, the engine caught and roared, and the Fiat was away and gone. And around the block, back, and again stopped at the curb!

The Good Whore of Palermo

This time the driver managed to keep the motor going, and a good-humored conversation continued for fifteen minutes or more. Eventually, perhaps certain commercial arrangements were made …

Now, surely I am not such a romantic that I will offer up the regular girl on this corner as the "good whore" of Palermo simply because she has a good heart when faced with a stalled car. No. Whoring is not, after all, a satisfactory living except for the poor of body or soul, and the good-hearted whore is generally a creation of the film industry. Also, at first glance, perhaps only God can truly identify a good heart. Later on that evening, however, God happened to pass through the piazza in the person of a heavy old mother leading two little children by either hand. I had the impression, at first, that she was going to ignore the younger woman and simply pass by. But then she slowed and gradually came to a halt. She turned, paused, looked. The old mother looked at the whore, then walked slowly up to her, and they talked quietly for a few minutes while the two children stood by her side. Then the mother quietly said her good-bye, preparing to walk on with the children, and at that moment she gave her own judgment. With the children still at her side, holding her two hands, the old woman leaned up and gently kissed the whore on one cheek. Then she kissed her on the other cheek. Then she slowly walked home with her two children to make the evening meal.

The story you have just read was first published, just as you see it, in *Mediterranean Stories* in 2000. It is included here primarily for the obvious reason. An unusual and true story of an old woman who touched—kissed—a young street prostitute at night on the streets of Palermo. This is perhaps sufficient reason ...

Parenthetically, there is a strange and perhaps wonderful aspect to this tale. *It greatly challenges the boundary between fiction and nonfiction.*

As you have just read it, this is absolutely nonfiction. Every bit of it was seen by human eyes. Pravda!

However! Watch what happens if one alters just two words in the last lines of this tale:

> With the children still at her side, holding her two hands, the old *grandmother* leaned up and gently kissed the whore on one cheek. Then she kissed the other cheek. Then she slowly walked home with her two *grandchildren* to make the evening meal.

There are many academics and many publishers who believe it matters, but no one on earth to my knowledge can tell you whether this altered version is fiction or nonfiction. Probably it is correct, the truth. But only God knows ...

Love at the Hotel Enosis

The Enosis is a dingy little hotel on Athinas Street in the Athens market district. The entrance is dimly lit at night, and the stairs to the second floor are steep and dreary. Nevertheless, the sidewalk in front of Enosis is a sort of force field that seems to grasp and draw passersby. Not only young men but occasionally an ancient, bent woman will change course on the sidewalk before the Enosis. They come close to the entrance and tilt their heads slightly *en passant,* glancing up the stairs. Because sometimes during the day, and at all possible hours of darkness, one or two women will be sitting on the stairs or the landing with their legs spread wide. The women are an advertisement. Perhaps they are not really there; perhaps they are somewhere else, trying to remember what it was like to be fifteen years old and happy. Their bodies, however, are white neon signs. The Enosis is a brothel.

It was Melina Mercouri, in *Never on Sunday,* who gave the U.S. its modern myth of the Good-Hearted Whore. Mercouri died in New York City a few years ago after a siege of cancer, and by chance I was in Athens when her body was flown back there for services. Far more than a movie star to the Greeks, she was a major political figure, revered for her opposition to the Greek dictatorship of 1967–1974. Very slowly, with many pauses, a wagon carried her closed coffin from the Metropolitan Cathedral through the center of Athens to her burial ground. This took a couple of hours, as I recall, and whenever the coffin moved ahead, a fountain of rose petals lofted high into the air from both sides of the roadway. If the carriage paused, the petals paused. When it resumed the journey, a soft cascade of red and pink and white petals floated above the fountain. This went on for two hours. Athens knows how to say good-bye to a beloved.

The Enosis Hotel is only about a seven-minute walk from the Metropolitan Cathedral—but at Enosis the good-hearted whore would be hard to identify. Nevertheless, the hotel is of some interest.

Enosis is an appropriate name for a brothel. In Greek it means to join two things together. Some of the women at the Enosis are attractive. Most are not. The men who go there are generally young and sometimes laughing, but more often stone-faced. Enosis is a lower-class affair, and cheap. My home in Athens, the Attalos Hotel, is only a few doors away. I have been passing the Enosis every so often for fifteen years. And when I do so I often think of the odd poverty of the English language in regard to the sexual act. It is said that the Eskimo have more than fifty words for different kinds of snow, and some agricultural people may have dozens of words for an especially important crop in its different stages. However, for the sexual act only a handful of English words are in common use and most of them are either zoological or obscene. An exception is "lovemaking," and imagination tells me that while humor is often made at the Enosis—and affection, cruelty, and sadness are commonly made—*to make love* may be rare in this place. Nevertheless, it may not be unknown.

As I passed by early one morning, at perhaps 7:30 or 8:00 a.m., one of the women was sprawled pitifully on the bottom steps of the stairway in plain sight of the street. She hardly even seemed a living human being. She lay there like a child's broken doll, or a rotten and discarded washcloth. The whore had been thrown out; she had reached an endpoint. She might as well have been lying in her grave. I could only speculate, but perhaps she had come to the Enosis destitute a few weeks or months before—and had now been scrapped.

Perhaps she had been told that morning that she must go. "You are stupid and homely, you can't smile or pretend to like the customers, you served *no one* last night. The food you eat is wasted. *Go.*" But there is no place to go. The Enosis is the bottom rung on the ladder of the human condition; below it there may be nothing but the abyss, and now she was crumpled at the edge. This was how she appeared to me, and to a Greek man passing by at the same moment.

He was a simple, strong, middle-aged working man in ordinary clothes on his way to work in the nearby market district. He saw the whore sprawled with her legs partly on the sidewalk. He slowed down to look at her and then walked up to the stairs and sat down. He sat on his haunches, resting easily. He looked at her. She did not move. He pulled from his pocket a pack of cigarettes, tapped one out, held out the pack toward her.

Then he spoke. I do not know a single word of what he said, but his was the most beautiful voice I have ever heard. He spoke in a soft rumble, very gently, softly, easily, without tension. He said … I know exactly what he said. His voice fell on the street like the down of a bird. "Don't worry. They can't ever do this to you again. Nobody will ever do this. Never this again. All the rest of your life … will be better. Only better. Now. Take the cigarette. Don't talk. Take the cigarette. I will light it. Then I am going to reach out and rub your shoulders. You will do whatever you need to do. Then, later, you must tell me what I will do to help. We must take care of each other."

What am I saying? What has this to do with the making of love? Only a madman—and a poet in the bargain, perhaps—would make a leap from this broken whore to … to what? Well, yes, perhaps only a mad poet:

Fire in the Ice Age

I thought Love lived in the hot sunshine,
But O, he lives in the moony light!
I thought to find Love in the heat of day,
But sweet Love is the comforter of night.

Seek Love in the pity of others' woe,
In the gentle relief of another's care,
In the darkness of night and the winter's snow,
In the naked and outcast, seek Love there.
—William Blake

The Critical Roles of Touch
Rev. Jeff Hale

Long before understanding anything about the meaning of love, a child feels loved through physical touch. Hugging and kissing a six-year-old as he or she leaves for school in the morning is a way of filling the child's emotional love tank, thus preparing him or her for a day of learning.

New research shows that the experience of being touched has direct and crucial effects on the growth of the body as well as the mind. While a warm touch is part of loving contact, research suggests that touch has an importance over and above other expressions of affection and that its presence, or absence, has consequences for the psychological and physical development of infants.

Dr. Tiffany Field, a psychologist at the University of Miami Medical School, has completed extensive studies on the importance of touch as it pertains to the growth and development of infants. Her work focused on the importance of touch itself, beyond that of merely being part of a parent's loving presence. Her findings may help explain the long-noted syndrome in which infants deprived of direct human contact grow slowly or even die.

In Field's research, premature infants who were massaged for fifteen minutes three times a day gained weight 47 percent faster than others who were left alone in their incubators, a standard practice in the past. The massaged infants also showed signs that their nervous systems were maturing more rapidly. According to Dr. Field, the infants became more active than other babies and more responsive to such things as a face or a rattle.

"The massaged infants did not eat more than the others," says Dr. Field. "Their weight gain seems due to the effect of contact on their metabolism." The infants who were massaged were discharged from the hospital an average of six days earlier than premature infants who were not massaged.

Eight months later, long after their discharge, the massaged infants did better on tests of mental and motor ability than the infants who were not and held on to their advantage in weight, according to a report by Dr. Field in *The Journal of Pediatrics.*

The standard policy in caring for premature infants has been a minimal-touch rule. Word of Dr. Field's findings and others that support them is leading to a change in this policy in many hospitals.

Dr. Field remarks, "In most parts of the world, people massage babies. Only in Western countries is this not a routine."

The importance of physical contact becomes most evident in a child's need for comfort and security. For instance, when a small child is frightened, the most effective way to calm him is for someone he trusts to hold him. Simply being there or reassuring him is not enough.

Children attempting new experiences, such as walking, riding a bike, or skating, all find comfort and courage from being held during the early attempts. When injured, a youngster desires the healing touch of a compassionate parent.

Physical touch is also an extremely powerful vehicle of communicating expressions of marital love. Holding hands, kissing, embracing, and of course, sexual intimacy are all ways of physically expressing emotional love to one's spouse. Without those physical expressions of closeness and affection, we feel unloved. With physical touch we feel secure in the love of our spouse.

There are times when it is almost instinctive and natural to hug another, and that is in times of crisis. It is then, more than at any other time, when we need to feel loved. We cannot always change events, but we can survive if we feel loved. And physical touch is a universal way of expressing that care and comfort.

In times of crisis, people don't really want explanations, words, sermons, or lectures! What they really want is just an indication that you care: maybe a hug or just someone to sit with them and hold their hand. The hug or other physical expression of caring will be remembered and appreciated far more than any words.

No matter the circumstances, no other aid is more comforting than that of the human touch.

The Unwanted

> I am someone alive after the Holocaust. It is essential that we, those living now, name ourselves as people who know what went before. That we mark our understanding of the effects of hatred … That we say that the hatred is not forgivable …
> —Mary Gordon, *Shadow Man*

Sad as it may be, most cultures—not all—have a despised underclass upon which most good people look down. That group may be a race, a religion, a different culture, or perhaps simply the tribe that lives in the next valley. In Ukraine in recent centuries, that underclass has been the Gypsy. The following stories touch upon the Gypsies of the first decade of the twenty-first century. As an American in Ukraine, I was looked down upon by many—not all—because I was openly friendly toward Gypsies. The Gypsies, especially the kids, often felt warmly toward me. Here are a few tales.

The Gypsy and the Guitar

Once upon a time in Ukraine, a tiny Gypsy boy in shabby winter clothes was given his first guitar. He was perhaps ten years old. When he stood the guitar up, it was nearly as tall as he was. I saw him walking near the river on the day he was given the guitar. He was wild with pride. He was so happy he could barely stand up. Mozart at his peak of achievement could not have been more joyful. Soon his parents had him playing in the streets of the Centrum with a beggar's cup in front of him. To my uneducated ear, his music meant little. His voice seemed guttural, harsh. But over the next months my friends told me that the little child, with both guitar and voice, had much talent and skill. He was good. My wife, who had mixed feelings toward many people not of her tribe, praised him highly.

One day I happened to have my camera with me and took a few photos of the little boy. They show him sitting on the pavement playing his guitar. The beggar's cup is in front of him, and there is snow on the pavement beyond. When the photographs came out nicely, I had one blown up to 30 x 40 cm. Occasionally I carried it with me in my daypack; if I saw the boy again, I would give it to him. The poor cannot afford cameras and film, and often they are happy with a photo. Then things got more interesting.

March 8 came on the cold winds of late winter. International Women's Day. Celebrated here with more than twenty-four hours of eating, drinking, and gift-giving, it is possibly the one day in this world when women are treated better than men. (*What* world do I have in mind? Perhaps all of it.) On March 8 I strolled down to the Centrum thinking, *If I find the child I will give him the photo, point to it, and say "Mama! Mama!"* Well, I found him at his usual spot. And standing quietly behind him was a small, shabby, subdued Gypsy woman. She looked quite poor. And, yes, it was Mama. I showed the blown-up photo to them. (The child was sitting at the same spot as in the photograph, wearing the same red cap and winter coat.) The two of them were smiling happily. I did not tarry; our only common languages were smiles and the photo. But as I turned away to leave, I saw the man standing behind me. And I saw in his eyes … what was in his heart. The man was perhaps forty. Lean, hungry face, not well off, his eyes filled with scorn and contempt. For me. For the Gypsies. For himself.

"*Fools,*" said his eyes. "Gypsy scum. *If only the Germans had stayed. If only they had stayed longer, it would have been* Auschwitz. Auschwitz. Auschwitz ..."

I understand. I understand the man, very well. I also hate. If it were not for the penalties, I would have killed him. When I later told my wife about the entire scene, she said,

"That is what I really hate. Not the Gypsies, but that man, men like that ..."

The Gypsy Girl

Spring came late in Uzhgorod that year, and March 17 was one of the first warm days. On Prospekt Svobodi the sun was bright, the air was balmy, and people were sitting happily at tables outside the cafes. Near the post office a music store had an outdoor loudspeaker playing rock music, and here I came upon a Gypsy child dancing on the sidewalk. She was wearing heavy, very dirty winter clothes. Her dark jacket was so massive that she looked a bit like a round little clown. She wore a heavy black cap and had a round, chubby little face. The girl was dancing by herself, her feet moving just a bit, arms out, swaying to the beat. And she wore a happy smile. She might have been fifteen.

As I walked toward her along the sidewalk, I think she saw my eyes on her. She pulled the black cap down over her face until the eyes were nearly hidden. Her eyes glittered under the edge of the cap, watching ... Then as I walked past, she came over and with a blank, expressionless face said,

"Kopek?"

I keep small coins in my coat pocket, and gave her those, but they were few and of little value. I passed on down the street. But then, after I'd gone a good ten meters beyond, I had a thought.

She's a nice child. The few kopeks, that was a little cheap. I think I'll make her happy. And I turned around and walked back. She was watching me. She saw me turn around, and she began smiling, and I was smiling, and the closer I got the wider grew the smile on the round little face. I gave her a two hryvnia note (all of forty cents). I noticed that her fingernails were chewed short and that her hands were very dirty. And her face, and her clothes, all filthy. And then—everything went out of control. The little girl threw her arms around me and gave me a huge hug. She was smiling wildly, her face full of joy, unspeakably happy (for the purchasing power of $2). Then, finally, she let go of my middle, reached up, and (to my mild horror) strongly pulled my head down and kissed me emphatically, twice on my right cheek. Then, smiling radiantly, she let me go. I ran away. (No, I walked away, fast.)

I walked toward the river, smiling from embarrassment. And then I saw the man sitting at a café table smiling at me and shaking his head. He was commiserating with me, that I'd been grabbed and kissed by that extremely dirty little Gypsy. Poor fellow. He'd never know, the poor man, he'd never know the mystery. Mystery? You don't see it. No. Of course not. You—all of you—you won't believe me. But it doesn't matter. At that moment, when I was kissed and hugged by that shabby little child of the street— and pitied by an onlooker—well, sorry, but it was the smile. At that moment *she was the most beautiful girl in the world. Absolutely screaming gorgeous. I'll remember her all my life.* William Blake knew her. He wrote about her:

> *Seek Love in the pity of other's woe*
> *In the gentle relief of another's care.*
> *In the darkness of night and the winter's snow,*
> *In the naked and outcast, seek Love there.*

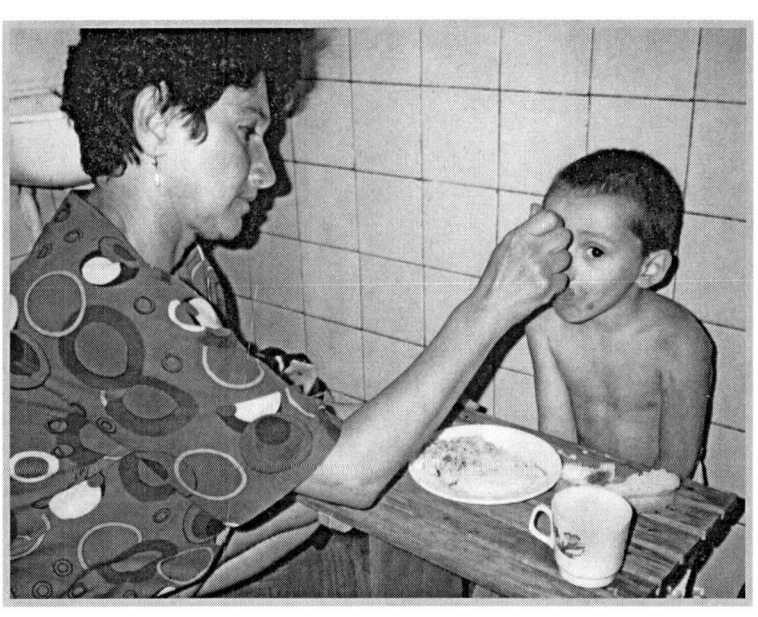

Natalia and Gypsy child. Photograph by the author.

Attitudes Toward the Gypsy in Southwest Ukraine

(Not fiction)

Although we share no common language, during my five years in Uzhgorod I was on friendly terms with a number of Gypsies. I soon learned that the majority of local people looked upon them with contempt. However, it was clear that this was not universal, and also clear that the Gypsies were often greatly respected for their musical skills.

My beloved wife, Natalia, committed suicide in June 2006. For months after that tragedy I was in much pain and extremely lonely. In my loneliness I thought of finding a woman companion (but did not act on the idea). However, on my street in Uzhgorod I often saw a middle-aged Gypsy woman who seemed very beautiful. Quite tall, slender, a magnificent hawk's face with a great smile, and at times beautifully dressed. And she smiled at me! Once she even kissed me briefly on the mouth! I idly remarked to a highly intelligent young university friend, a frequent companion, that if I publicly associated with a Gypsy woman, I myself would probably be outcast. Much to my curiosity his response was a brief, "Not in all circles." A few days later I learned the history behind that remark. I spent an evening with his family and heard a remarkable family history. The bare bones of the story are as follows.

The father was raised in a medium-sized town in the Carpathians, one with diverse and tolerant inhabitants. There were several nationalities, diverse political beliefs, and a respected Gypsy community. He had been raised with tolerant attitudes. When he was born his mother did not have sufficient breast milk, and he had been breast-fed by a Gypsy woman. Enough said!

My friend's mother, a very warm-hearted and kind soul, also had her story. In the hospital where her son was born, a Gypsy woman had abandoned a baby—and my friend's mother had breast-fed the Gypsy child.

Yes, enough said.

Let it be said: In Uzhgorod, early in the twenty-first century, I was kissed twice on the mouth by the unwanted Gypsy. A bit akin to a kiss from a Black woman in Mississippi in 1950. (One of them was gorgeous. In 2009—I'd marry her in a minute.)

Do justice, love kindness, walk humbly with your God. Jesus said nothing about shoes. He said nothing else at all ... If you want more, I refer you back to that passage from the greatest poet of the English language, William Blake:

In the naked and outcast, seek Love there.

Alone by the Fire in the Ice Age

Many years ago I knew a woman whom I shall call Susan, and later knew her daughter (I'll call her Debbi) quite well. Both are good people, quiet and intelligent. Both, however, had difficult early lives. Recently I received a letter from Susan, who is now over eighty years old. It contained the following lines, in response to Nowlan's poem on page ix.

> *I'm ... having a problem about physical touching.*
> I have no women friends ...
> I've been close, or nearly, to four men in different degrees ...
> *I've had to teach myself to sit alone by that fire in the Ice Age.*
> With [an] old friend, we developed a signature to letters:
> —*two worlds that intersected and overlapped—a little.*
> When there are two people ... there is always one left. We live alone inside our bodies.

I first really knew Susan's daughter Debbi when the girl was about fourteen years old. She visited my home in Berkeley one summer, and I vividly remember a scene in front of my fireplace. We lit a fire one evening, and there was a thick, soft rug on the floor, and our two Weimaraner dogs were lying back to back before the fire. There was a foot or so of space between them. The daughter looked down on them, looked for several seconds … then flung herself down between them and wrapped her arms around them. Debbi lay there hugging the dogs for quite a long time.

Three years later Debbi again visited me in Berkeley during the summer. Her bedroom was a second-floor porch at the back of the house, where the sun poured in each morning. One morning I needed to speak to her about something or other, and I knocked gently on her door. A cheerful voice said,

"Come in." I opened the door, looked in, and saw Debbi lying on her back and looking up with a happy smile on her face.

"Hi!" she said. She looked extremely pleased with herself. And … her arms were wrapped around two young boys who were lying on either side. The boys were silent and their eyes were closed. Debbi, however, could not possibly have been happier with her small fire in the ice age … She was smiling as if she owned the whole world.

Beyond Touch

He:

I was sitting on a concrete bench near a corner of Prospekt Svobodi when the woman walked past. She was young and homely and so drunk she could barely stand. She looked at me. Walked past. Came back. And sat down beside me. She was so drunk she could barely sit there without falling over. She looked at me with her eyes, and the eyes were dead. The eyes did not want anything.

I have heard—they have told me—that the eyes are the windows to the soul. But I looked into her eyes. And there was nothing. Nothing. I think this must be the hardest country in the world.

She sat there. Said a few very slow words. We had no common tongue. I said a few words. I said,

"I'm sorry."

She replied, not knowing what the words meant,

"I'm sorry."

We were both sorry.

I gently rubbed my hand up and down between her shoulders. Her bruised face said nothing. Her dead eyes said nothing. She was gone. I felt helpless. I did not want her sitting there beside me; I could not help her and she made me feel sad.

What could she possibly have wanted? Soon I went away.

This brief episode occurred in Uzhgorod, Ukraine, in October of 2003.

I am not really sure that it merits a place in this book. But ... the woman was beyond touch ...

After we separated, I was a bit haunted by the poor soul, and I imagined a few of the thoughts that might have passed through her head …

She:
    I will tell you what I wanted. Listen …
    I wanted a different life.
    I wanted to sit next to someone. Anyone. And not have them go away.
    I wanted to be "sorry." What is "sorry"?
    I don't know what I wanted. Maybe I wanted to be "sorry."
    After he left I walked across Prospekt Svobodi to the Hungarian cemetery and went to sleep between the tombstones. I wanted never to wake up. There was no tombstone for me. Not even that. I tried. I looked. There was no stone with my name. Not even that …
    "I'm sorry." I'm sorry …
    Goodbye …

10/12/03

The Touched Face

During the free-thinking period of 1965 to 1980, "growth movement" or "human potential" workshop groups of many kinds were an accepted part of Northern California culture. Many of these groups sometimes worked in the nude, and massage groups always did.

Between 1971 and 1980, I made a comfortable living in my large old home in the Berkeley hills running divorce support groups. After these groups and my large living room–dining room working floor space became well known, other men and women in the group movement often used my home for their one- or two-day workshops. It was a period of cultural revolution.

One man in the region, George Downing, became famous for writing a classic book—the first—on what we knew as "long stroke" massage (not hard and penetrating). By chance we were close neighbors, and in the early 1970s he ran many massage workshops in my home. (In fact, as I recall, many of the illustrations for his book were done in my home.)

We need a brief description of the way Downing's workshops were set up. He would offer a one-day Saturday workshop for perhaps sixteen to twenty people. I was usually a guest as part of my compensation. Typically there were morning and afternoon teaching sessions, and a long break for a leisurely potluck dinner of wonderful food. (Each person brought an item.)

And then, from perhaps eight until late into the night, we would practice what we had been taught. People would pair off in couples (both same sex and opposite sex) and practice on one area of the body. Always working in the nude. Then a new pairing and another area of the body. Always working on the thick, soft rugs on the floor. When darkness had fallen I built a large wood fire in the fireplace and the lights were turned low… (I tell you, for any man or woman who loves to be touched, this was the life of royalty!)

One last remark regarding Downing's teaching routine in these one-day workshops: Work one area of the body at a time, front and back, often beginning on the back and legs. Then work on the front of the body, as I recall. *And then, the last area of the body to be massaged was the face.* Dear reader, if you have not experienced a thorough face massage at the hands of an expert, *my words will be useless.* No man can do justice to this with words. In my opinion, a world-class writer can do justice to almost any human experience. But not this.

Downing taught approximately as follows. To work on the face: one person lies on the rug; the other kneels on the floor above the head of the receiver. Begin at the side of the face and neck, and briefly work around and under the nape of the neck. (The back of the neck at the base of the skull is extremely sensitive due to the many cranial and cervical nerves leaving the brain in that region.) Then work under the chin and slowly around the mouth, both below and above. Always working from the side toward the midline of the face and the nose.

Working very slowly and gently for possibly a half hour, finally we arrive at the eyes. And the massage of the eyes *must be done very gently and with extreme care.* I would guess that perhaps most of us are not fully aware of this, but the eye region is extremely sensitive. As we were taught, one gently massages the area around the eye. And finally, at the very end of a day of great sensitivity and openness to the human touch, very slowly and gently one slides the forefingers inside the sockets of the skull and gently curls the forefingers around the eye socket. There is enough space within the socket to permit a gentle forefinger. Which allows the eyeball itself to receive gentle pressure.

As I glance back over these words, written in April 2009, I realize that you, the reader, might think the story of the touched face is now pretty much done. *No.* This is only the introduction to a breathtaking moment.

Listen carefully. I myself probably would not entirely believe these words if I had not experienced this. It was a warm, soft late evening in Berkeley, California, perhaps in 1974. Eight or nine couples were exchanging massage—the end of a long day of a Downing workshop. I knelt on the floor of my own living room with my back to a warm, low fire in the fireplace. In front of me on the rug, lying on her back with her head at my knees, lay an extremely relaxed and beautiful woman.

She was a stunning, tall, slender, arrogant blonde Frenchwoman, now married to an American. (He was absent.) For everyone in the room it had been a day of much pleasure. Probably we were all quite relaxed and open to the gift of touch. I had nearly completed our routine by working gently on her face, and now quite softly touched the area of her eyes. Gently, gently, I then touched and stroked inside her eye sockets.

Suddenly her lovely body stirred, and her flat and relaxed abdomen began to stir and then fluttered wildly for a few moments! Then, at brief intervals her stomach rose and fluttered twice again. The woman had had three orgasms.

Until that moment this woman had had no interest in me whatever. But now, after a few moments of mutually stunned silence, she stood up. Shaken. Shocked into silence. I recall that she stood silently for a few moments. And then, staring at me in the soft light of the fire, she spoke. Softly.

"Do you have a bedroom upstairs?"

I did not. In honesty, I cannot recall the reason for my refusal. I had a room, yes, but I said no. She left minutes later. I never saw her again.

Since I am seventy-nine, I can afford to tell you a truth that few people know. There are at least nine different points on the body through which a woman can experience orgasm. The human face is extraordinarily sensitive to touch …

Pravda.

Sérife

Simena, Turkey, has no road, no cars, no policemen or doctors, no post office, no dogs—well, almost none. Simena has had electricity and phones only since about 1985. Everything comes from the sea, beginning perhaps four thousand years ago with the Minoans and then the Phoenicians. Only the nomad Turks came over the land. Every morning the bread boat comes around nine from Üçağız (do not try to pronounce words with this many wiggles). The golden bread, long loaves stacked vertically in bright blue and red crates, stands like piles of yellow firewood against the flat deep blue sea. Then, several days a week, the vegetable boats come from Üçağız. All day big boats and little skiffs bring tanks of water, which is laboriously piped or carried in large jugs up into the village. The jugs are sturdy plastic, but their handles are identical in shape to those of 2,500-year-old earthenware amphorae. The shards of amphorae now lie all about, buried beneath the packed soil of the village. The day-tour *gulets*—luxury motorboats—bring tourists and easy money from Kas or Kale, then carry the tourists away by dusk. In the night there are no sounds but the distant rustle of laughter, the rooster, the little owls. The acetylene torches in the sky—are stars.

In Simena life is slow and seamless, of a piece. People asked me, "Why don't you live here?" Good God. I told Nesrim, "I will if I can find a Turkish wife." She said, "I will try to find you one." Why would I think, even for a second, of staying in such a tiny place? Because, very simply, the people of this village have treated me with unimaginable kindness. Most tourists come, race to the castle above the village, hustle back to their boats, and in an hour or so they go away. So sad. I was there for twelve days and people asked—"Why don't you stay?"

Why might I stay? Two clear reasons. First, I am an old man, and Simena is the only place I have ever known where, if I stayed and died there, a village would cry at my grave. And second, this is the only place where a beautiful girl fell in love with me without speaking a word. I think sweet Sérife spoke only Turkish, but this will not stop a young girl in matters of the heart. On my first day here, a little hand took mine and led me through a mob of tourists, through a restaurant, and out a low concrete quay, then tried to lead me onto a gulet. I explained to her—*we weren't invited*. She found both the concept and my English incomprehensible, but ever since that day Sérife has owned me.

She sat often in my lap. Each time her mother took her away, she came back. (She was only two and a half years old.) And then one day I walked by her parents' one-room home to find her in the path with a soft cloth rope around her waist, the other end anchored to a stone wall. The mother works; and in her explorations, Sérife is as mobile and fanatic as a raccoon. So—a leash. The little girl took one look, saw me—and wordless, tottered over to my bare legs. She wrapped both arms tightly against my knees and buried her face against the skin of my thighs. And prepared to stand there forever. Her entire tiny being radiated the sad, incomprehensible, new and sometimes horrible discoveries of the tiny: first, not-invited-to-the-gulet—and now *they-tied-me-up, they-tied-me-up, they ... tied ... me ... up ...*

Sérife is an old and sober little soul.

The Farthest Shore: Touch, Evil, and the Forbidden …

> All living souls welcome whatever they are able to cope with. All else they ignore, or pronounce to be monstrous and wrong, or deny to be possible.
> —George Santayana

We are speaking here about touching, holding, *human contact* and the intolerant attitudes of many Americans toward those who openly display physical intimacy. Intolerance not only of intimacy taking place before them but in many forms of art, even art by the hands of some of the very greatest artists in all of history!

This is profoundly a cultural matter, of course. What is acceptable in one society or one century may be utterly condemned in another. Attitudes toward nudity, or toward prostitution, are classic.

Before we deal with examples of the forbidden, a few more words about my fellow Americans: it seems to me that much of the matter simply lies in the ignorance of most toward other cultures. *Approximately 80 percent of Americans do not have a foreign passport, and many who do hold a passport never leave the Americas.* To me, this is almost a cultural catastrophe. Most Americans are so sheltered from the harsher realities of human existence that I doubt they could even give a proper definition of the term *evil*.

Evil? What is evil …

Three Ancient Dancers: Evil, Pragmatism, and Human Decency

I lived in Uzhgorod, Ukraine, from 2001 until my beautiful fifty-two-year-old Ukrainian wife, a linguistic genius, was devoured by vodka and committed suicide in 2006. At one point Natalia told me flatly that I could never understand the Russians! (An American journalist once lived in Moscow for twenty years and still said on departure, "I don't understand these people at all.") But finally, Natalia said to me, "If you want to understand them, read Dostoyevsky, and read Lermontov's *A Hero For Our Time.*"

Anyone who reads these pages might well meditate afterward on the nature of evil, as well as the nature of human nobility. Certain Slavonic writers pay a good bit of attention to evil. In Ukraine at the change of millennia, the primary concern of most people is simply survival. Their approach is essentially pragmatic: whatever will feed my family, this I will do. My suspicion is that I am witness to a performance between three ancient dancers: evil, pragmatism, and human decency. Therefore I think often of this remarkable passage from Mikhail Lermontov's *A Hero for Our Time* touching on the relationship between pragmatism and evil:

> I could not help being struck by the capacity of the Russian to adapt himself to the customs of that people among which he happens to be living. I do not know whether this trait of the mind deserves blame or praise, but it attests to his incredible flexibility and the presence of that lucid common sense that *pardons evil* [emphasis mine] wherever it recognizes its necessity or the impossibility of its abolishment.

When I first came to Uzhgorod I lived for several months in the lower-class Radvanka district sometimes known as Gypsytown. I was robbed, and the product was the story "Hunger." (I was not robbed by a Gypsy.) Then I moved to a flat in the Prospekt Svobodi and Squirrel Market neighborhood. This is a representative cross section of the city. In a sense, it is middle-class Uzhgorod, but in reality it is a mix of all classes. The rich may shop there, and those of limited means live there, as do many poor people. Those of the economic bottom scavenge at the Squirrel Market, beg and steal there, drink and die there. I lived next to the market from late 2001 through 2003.

Dear friends: live next to the starving and dying souls near the Squirrel Market, and read Lermontov, and you will begin to meditate upon the nature of evil. Read the following *true story,* and then meditate upon the Slavs of the twentieth century.

"The Americans won't understand. Tell them about the Good Fairy of Leningrad. Tell them! Do it! They read about the Slavs as a good and decent people suffering under an intolerable history. Goddammit, they won't have the slightest idea what 'intolerable history' means. Go ahead, tell them about Leningrad. Try to tell them, at least try. All you can do is fail. Do it! Tell them what it means to have an intolerable history …"

During the German siege of Leningrad, a Good Fairy lived in the city with her three Fairy Children. They were all starving. Soon they would all die. During the starving time, men were selling meat pies in the streets. One could be bought for the price of a gold ring, or a bit of jewelry. The pies were filled with the flesh of a rat, or cat, or dog, or human being. The Good Fairy would not buy them. Finally she and the three little Fairy Children were sitting on the edge of their open graves. What could she do? What?? The Good Fairy killed one of her Fairy Children. She fed a good meal to the other two. Then she went mad.

I showed this little fairy tale to a young woman of Uzhgorod, and she said,

"I know a hundred stories like that from the nineteen twenties and thirties. It happened here in Ukraine, in the villages … *It happened here."*

The rest of this chapter shall touch briefly upon the works of three great artists. As you read these brief accounts, my purpose should become clear.

Constantine Cavafy

The magnificent Alexandrian Greek poet of the twentieth century, Constantine Cavafy, wrote of the voluptuous darker culture of Alexandria, Egypt. Some of his poetry was published during his lifetime, but not one volume of poems. Why?

> **On the Stairs**
> *As I was going down those ill-famed stairs*
> *you were coming in the door, and for a second*
> *I saw your unfamiliar face and you saw mine.*
> *Then I hid so you wouldn't see me again,*
> *and you hurried past me, hiding your face,*
> *and slipped inside the ill-famed house*

where you couldn't have found sensual pleasure
  any more
than I did.

And yet the love you were looking for, I had to give you;
the love I was looking for—so your tired,
knowing eyes implied—you had to give me.
Our bodies sensed and sought each other;
our blood and skin understood.

But, flustered, we both hid ourselves.

The following poem was published and shown to friends in several versions. This is probably the most honest ...

The Bandaged Shoulder
... the bandage came undone and a little blood ran.

I did it up again, taking my time
over the binding; he wasn't in pain
and I liked looking at the blood.
It was a thing of my love, that blood.

When he left, I found, in front of his chair,
a bloody rag, part of the dressing,
a rag to be thrown straight into the garbage;
and I put it to my lips
and kept it there a long while—
the blood of love against my lips.

"Where could I better live?" he once remarked, in the worldly tone we recognize from his verse. "Under me is a house of ill repute, which caters to the needs of the flesh. Over there is the church, where sins are forgiven. And beyond is the hospital, where we die."

> *The crime occurred last night*
> *around ten. The paper, rightly,*
> *abhorred the murder, but typically,*
> *displayed its complete disdain*
> *for the reprobate life of the victim,*
> *for the corrupt individual.*
>
> *He read. The paper made an error,*
> *it wouldn't have been ten, but much later.*
> *They were together until twelve*
> *(the first time—they barely knew each other*
> *by sight) in a room that was*
> *half hotel, half brothel.*
> *It noted the details of the wound ...*
> *The motive was attempted blackmail ...*
> *Mechanically he read about*
> *the indignation that the reporter felt*
> *about the crime; and immediately afterward*
> *about his disdain for the depraved victim.*
>
> *His disdain ... And he, mourning inwardly,*
> *recalled the sweet lips; the exquisitely*
> *white, sublime flesh that he hadn't kissed enough.*

William Blake

William Blake (1757–1827) might be considered the greatest poet of the English language in all of history. He was also, of course, a magnificent painter and printmaker. With no further comments, here are poems that speak for themselves ...

A Little Girl Lost
Children of the future age,
Reading this indignant page,
Know that in a former time,
Love, sweet Love, was thought a crime.

A prophet and social critic, William Blake was one of the most strikingly original poets of the Romantic age. Writing at a time of strict social convention and religious conformity, he spoke out against all restriction of human freedom. His belief in the power of the imagination, the supremacy of the emotions—even anger—and the need for free, open communication was the guiding principle of his poetry.

Blake was saved by his anonymity. In his prophetic writings he is free: free of all the inhibitions and distortions of publication and performance ("The outward Ceremony is Antichrist"). As he realized that his works were unlikely to be seen, they become ever more pure and true. They may be the purest poems we shall ever find, utterly unfettered by the chains of audience and publisher.

"I know of no other Christianity and of no other Gospel than the liberty, both of body and mind, to exercise the divine arts of imagination."

Gnomic Verses, VII
Love to faults is always blind;
Always is to joy inclin'd,
Lawless, wing'd and unconfin'd,
And breaks all chains from every mind.

Deceit to secrecy confin'd
Lawful, cautious and refin'd;
To anything but interest blind,
And forges fetters for the mind.

Michelangelo

Michelangelo (1475–1564) was perhaps the greatest artist who ever lived. He was a genius in several different media; sculpture and painting are perhaps the best known. But he was apparently cast into disgrace and relative obscurity by the Catholic Church in his last years. The reasons for this relate to religious divisions, according to recent interpretations. However, one of the real issues is said to be the nudity displayed in many of his greatest works. Nudity!

At the risk of going from the sublime to the ridiculous, let me just add that in the Year of Our Lord 2009, in Corvallis, Oregon, a woman may be scolded for breast-feeding her baby in a public place. Not for nudity, you understand—one may not see her breasts. She simply commits an act that is seen as an intimacy. A great number of my fellow citizens may not be aware of this, but in many cultures in the world a woman's breasts are not given any erotic significance whatever. They are, God help us all, simply seen as quite helpful for the feeding of infants.

Angel from the North

I first heard of Anna Abramenko from a Turkish gallery owner in Istanbul, a man with whom I sometimes drank cay (tea) almost daily. One morning Tugay spoke of a Russian prostitute named Anna. On two evenings he had paid for her services. But then Anna had said to him,

"Tugay, I want you to be my friend. I don't take money from you anymore—sometimes you can sleep with me, but no money. I want you for friend."

This story struck me as just a bit unusual; it implied a woman in a hard business who still, perhaps, had an open heart. Then Tugay told me that Anna spoke English very well, and in fact spoke six languages. Since I am extremely stupid with any tongue but my own, this impressed me no end. And then I thought, *why a prostitute?* With six languages one can find gainful employment of other sorts in the City of the Heart's Desire. I am a teller of stories, and this woman spoke English. And so I asked to meet Anna.

"Why?" she asked Tugay suspiciously. "Why does he want to meet me?" Tugay put me on his mobile phone, and the voice at the other end was brief and edgy, but we made an appointment to meet for lunch the next day.

I waited in front of the Agia Sofia. Turkish street hustlers have the sharpest noses in the world. They sniffed the air around me. "What do you want? Help with telephones? A woman? Carpets?" When I said "Yok (no)," to all of them, yok, yok, one looked at me carefully and said, "Sexy papa." Och! Moments after this unlikely remark from a street hustler, Anna arrived for our meeting.

She was quite beautiful when she smiled. And although we had never met, she smiled warmly when our eyes connected across the tram tracks of Divan Yolu. She was bright blonde, wore red lipstick on her large mouth, was handsomely dressed, and strode easily across the boulevard toward me on five-inch heels. She wore her clothes as if they were her skin, as if she would competently handle anything life sent her way. She probably could—she was a tough Slav. We shook hands and went down the hill toward the Magnaura Café for lunch.

Anna, it turned out, was twenty-four and from Murmansk, Russia. And since that city is a significant element in her story, let us briefly go there. Murmansk is one of the ends of the earth, a large city not far from the Arctic Circle. A drab, grim, and broken mix of military bases, manufacturing, and crumbling apartment houses of which David Shipler said in his book *Russia*,

> … it never sees the sun in the depth of winter. The perpetual darkness is softened only for a few hours across the middle of the day, when the sun hovers just below the horizon …
>
> An icy wind … rips in from the water, driving needles of frozen mist stinging against the skin. Districts of apartment houses were built in huge horseshoe-shaped configurations carefully positioned to form solid walls against the relentless winter wind; inside this shelter … schools and playgrounds were situated.

In perhaps 1975, a tiny girl named Anna Abramenko was born into a privileged family in this dark and bitter world. Her father was an important manufacturer; her mother raised five children, earning a Soviet medal for superior motherhood.

Anna was well educated and eventually became fluent in six languages. Clearly, this was not a child of poverty—but what remained for her at eighteen? Her answer, if it is to be believed: almost nothing. A dead-end secretary job. Little prospect of a decent marriage and children. Hideous climate. Russia was on the way down; Murmansk was a wasteland. What remained was ice-cold, savage wind, depression, vodka, suicide, darkness. The young Anna looked at her prospects and decided to resist her fate. She would go south. But *how?*

Anna is now my friend. As I know her today, at twenty-five she is an intelligent woman, but when I first met her, I took her to be a woman of limited ambition. (How stupid of me.) When she was eighteen and living in Murmansk, she had to my knowledge only one ambition—and only one asset with which to further that ambition. She wanted to be warm. She wanted the South. And in trade for it, she had only her beauty. If she sold it, all would know, and she would be an outcast. Anna shook with fear for two weeks, fear at what she was determined to do. Then, with open eyes and hard ambition, Anna went to a man she knew in a nightclub and arranged her first customer. And since he was the first, the go-between made special arrangements.

"Anna, your man is _____. You know his name, he is a famous Soviet general. On this piece of paper is his address, and the date and time you must go there. He said to tell you his servants will prepare a special dinner, a feast for the two of you. Then he will give you a tour of his home—it is full of very beautiful art and a splendid collection of icons. You will be very well treated. And you will spend the night."

Anna knocked on that door at the appointed hour, trembling with fear of the unknown. She was met at the door by the old general wearing a luxurious robe, but his eyes were filled not with desire, only with exhaustion. He invited her in quite politely and then apologized for a change in plans. He had just returned from a long and difficult day at work, he was extremely tired, and he was on his way to his bedroom. He was sorry. He regretted. But his need was to sleep. Anna was to go to the kitchen, he said, where she would be fed a dinner adequate for a king. His servants would care for her. Then she was welcome to explore the house, look at his beautiful collections. Then, when she was properly nourished with food and wine and the surroundings, she should come to his room.

Anna did as she was told, and perhaps an hour later knocked on the bedroom door. She had told me she had shaken for weeks, and one assumes she was still shaking, unless the wine were sufficient for the reality of the evening. But—what a reality! Anna knocked and knocked again. No answer. She entered. A gorgeous bed, a splendid room, a silver bucket of ice and champagne by the bed. And an old man deep in sleep … What must she do?!? Who was she to do … anything?! Finally she decided she should waken the old man. She shook him gently. Then a bit harder. It is no use—he is deeply asleep, the sleep of dead exhaustion. What must she do?!? She has orders, but she might as well try to wake up a parked Mercedes. Dear reader, all I know—all Anna ever told me—I now tell to you. Anna cast her anxious, confused, and perhaps wine-softened eyes about the room. In one corner was a beautifully covered sofa bed, or something of the sort. Imagine now, if you will, a scene from theater: a beautiful eighteen-year-old girl walks to the corner bed. With her back turned to you, she throws off her clothes. You have a most brief view of the back of her beautiful body. Then she crawls under the covers, pulls them over her head—and as the curtain comes down on Act I in Murmansk, Anna goes to sleep. By herself.

At the Magnaura Café, back in Istanbul, Anna and I had a long and satisfying lunch. We spent probably three hours on introductions. Anna was indeed fluent in English. She was well-educated, had read a good bit, and in fact had written some poetry. (This she had *no* intention of showing me, she said.) At one point she looked at me thoughtfully and said, "You are a writer. I should watch myself with you."

After leaving Murmansk, Anna had spent a couple of years working in different parts of the Balkan peninsula with a Russian friend. Then the two of them had come to Istanbul. If she is to be believed, she has always worked selectively and with great care. And somehow has retained a human heart.

After lunch we walked up the hill to the benches around the fountain near Sultanahmet Mosque. We sat quietly in the gentle glow of the mid-afternoon sun. Soft and quiet was the day. Warm was the air, and filled with the music of autumn—a rustle of falling leaves, the faint sound of the touching hands of courting children, the scratch of a crow's beak on a crust of bread. I gave Anna a copy of my book of stories. We spoke of friendship, and of what friendship might mean. We spoke briefly of the possibility of the bed, and Anna said, "It's too soon to talk of that." Finally she wrote her complete name on a scrap of paper and added two mobile phone numbers. "The first is the number my customers use," she said. "The second is for my friends. Almost nobody has that number." She told me to use the second and handed me the slip of paper. We parted at four o'clock in the soft, late and slanting light, with my mind filled with curiosity and heart improbably touched.

A few days later she told a friend that she had read passages in my book and almost cried. She did not, however, want me to think she was sentimental. She was not, said Anna.

During the following days we spoke often about our lives,

and during one of our conversations Anna said that as a child she thought often about death. I am going to die, she thought, I am going to die. I don't want to die. Her mother had reassured Anna that when she was older this would not seem to matter so much. Not a matter for concern. But no Russian mother would tell her child that she would never die.

Many days later, after a growing friendship, under Constantine's Wall in the City of the Heart's Desire we found a small low-ceilinged room facing east to the sea. We could see Asia and watched the full moon of November rise over it. We listened to the gulls that fly at night under the full moon. The warm soft air, the moonlight, the cries of the gulls, the faint noise from the streets below, all this washed through our window and onto our bed. We made love in ways that no sane man would ever share with a prostitute. Anna responded passionately, joyfully. Then we slept.

Our bed was just beneath the window, and all through the night the full moon washed over Anna's blanket and her white skin and washed her clean while she slept. Anna is afraid of death. Anna has a good and warm heart. Anna loves to play billiards, and when she does she leans over the table as intently as any bird of prey over a mouse. Anna sometimes makes love for money, but she will not take money from her friends. Anna has her life ahead of her and she will be okay. For Anna there is time enough for love.

You have just read a brief tale about the Anna I knew for a few days in an Istanbul October. But during the following year I learned more about this lively and unusual girl. And our story is not quite done. For one thing, while Anna was in Murmansk she had studied some of the more aggressive martial arts for more than a decade. For another, she had jumped out of airplanes eighteen times. Anna, it would seem, is a deliberate risk-taker, an adrenaline addict, the sort of soul who demands—at all costs—intensity, not boredom.

Also, from one October to the next Anna made radical changes in both her plans and her appearance. A year later, gone were the bright blonde hair and sharp clothes. We met again near Agia Sophia—and I might never have recognized the college kid in jeans with short black hair. Only her smile, her sensual mouth, and her laughter were the same.

"Now I am no longer doing the work," she said. "I am taking a one-year course in hotel management, studying Spanish, and probably will work in a hotel in Spain or South America." She seemed enormously excited about her studies and was apparently working quite seriously at them. Evidently there had been a metamorphosis. This would not be easy. Her studies may lag, hotel work may be routine. She may run short of funds. Old friends may invite her to go sailing—and then one may offer her a hundred-dollar bill to go down in the cabin. But Anna Abramenko is my friend, and I wish for her whatever she wishes for herself.

At the end of the millennium there was a happy turning point in Anna's story. In Istanbul she had said more than once that she felt without a home in the world. Apparently, when she had left Murmansk, her family and friends knew full well that she had chosen the life of a prostitute. Apparently, Anna was sure that she was outcast and would be ignored or greeted with contempt if she returned. However, in the bitter December depths of a Murmansk winter, the prodigal daughter came home and was greeted with joy and a loving Christmas celebration. All those who had loved her, loved her still. She was still wanted. She still had a home in the world. Her sister was overjoyed to see her. When she departed, her mother told her, "You are the best daughter in the world!" For Anna Abramenko there was time enough for love. Her God has told her so.

And now there is one last thing. Like most of us, she can change her mind. If you recall, she *swore* she would *never* show me her poetry. Anna was emphatic on that point! But now it is a new millennium, and look here!!! She handed me scraps of paper with four of her poems. And one of them, which I now share with you, contains one line that for me has all the poetic music in the world.

> When Fate gives me
>   enjoyment of a calm night—
> When in the morning I'll not
>   burn my poem—
> When new day does not turn
>   into an ordinary evening—
> When I do not make mistakes—
>   then I shall be
>   only a shadow …

We all need friends. We all need the same things, really; we all have the same hungers and fears. It seems to me that beyond a doubt, beyond any possible doubt, life is very beautiful, death is an illusion, hunger is very real, none of us has seen God—and none of this should be seen as a matter for any great concern … after all,

You are not yet gone.
We are still here.
Anna will survive and, I believe, prosper.

> *Do learn to see that life is marvelous. And not in a year, not in a hundred years. Now.*
> *—Anna*

The last time I saw Anna in Istanbul might have been in 2000. And, of course, by then she was no longer working as a prostitute. When we parted she gave me a slip of paper with her new e-mail address. It was

    Annaxxxx69@hotmail.com.

"Anna," I said in a mildly scolding tone, "Hotmail? That's to be expected, but sixty-nine? No, Anna, that's too much!"

"No, you don't understand," said she in a tone that suggested that I was a bit stupid.

"Sixty-nine is the latitude of Murmansk, where I was born."

I keep thinking that it's too good to be true. I keep checking the globe. Latitude 69 goes right through Murmansk.

Pravda.

The Price of Experience: a summing up

> *What is the price of Experience? do men buy it for a song?*
> *Or wisdom for a dance in the street? No, it is bought with*
>   *the price*
> *Of all that a man hath—his house, his wife, his*
>   *children.*
> *Wisdom is sold in the desolate market where none come to*
>   *buy,*
> *And in the wither'd field where the farmer plows for bread*
>   *in vain.*
> —William Blake

William Blake is the most powerful voice in all of the history of the English language. It is pointless, I think, to chatter about his arts—in all forms—compared to those of the greatest of the Italians, the Greeks, or the Russians. But I would argue that among writers, craftsmen of the language, he stands alone in the English tongue.

Why do I think this? I am no academic; the university has never heard my name. But read the poem at the top of this page. Then read it again. It is but one of hundreds. Read it again, and then look at me!

I have been a moderate success in four different professions, and highly recognized in two. I have seen twenty-five countries on four continents, and written of them. I have had four wives (three divorces and a suicide) and four children. I have made love to perhaps 150 different women—damned few of them a one-night stand, of which I'd be ashamed.

I have spent time with several Nobel Prize winners, and

with two men who helped to build the atomic bomb. And with men you have heard of: Timothy Leary, for example, has been a guest in my home. (When one moves from one profession and city to another, all is forgotten. But life is so much richer.)

What is the point of all this loose talk? I have published seven books in three languages. So?

My experience of life has been extremely rich. And my experience has cost me my house, my wives, and my children, who will not speak to me.

> Blake: *It is bought with the price of all that a man hath — his house, his wife, his children.*

This not merely a fine and beautiful poem. It is more than that ...

Epilogue

Unison Prayer of Confession

We thank you, God of wisdom and grace, for calling us into your church to be your people. We have gathered, O Holy One, to hear and be heard, *to touch and be touched*. In mercy and love, you have reached out to us in Jesus Christ *and touched us* with your transforming Spirit. Now we turn toward you, seeking to love as we have been loved. For our brokenness, we seek your healing. For our hardness of heart, we seek your grace. Empower us now to worship and serve you, walking gently on this earth, through the grace of Jesus the Christ. Amen.

Epistle to Be Left in the Earth

...It is colder now,
        there are many stars,
                we are drifting
North by the Great Bear,
        the leaves are falling,
The water is stone in the scooped rocks,
                to southward
Red sun grey air:
        the crows are
Slow on their crooked wings,
            the jays have left us:
Long since we passed the flares of Orion.
Each man believes in his heart he will die.
Many have written last thoughts and last letters.
None know if our deaths are now or forever:
None know if this wandering earth will be found.

We lie down and the snow covers our garments.
I pray you,
    you (if any open this writing)
Make in your mouths the words that were our names.
I will tell you all we have learned,
            I will tell you everything:

Fire in the Ice Age

The earth is round,
                there are springs under the orchards,
The loam cuts with a blunt knife,
                beware of
Elms in thunder,
                the lights in the sky are stars —
We think they do not see,
                we think also
The trees do not know nor the leaves of the grasses hear us:
The birds too are ignorant.
                Do not listen.
Do not stand at dark in the open windows.
We before you have heard this:
                they are voices:
They are not words at all but the wind rising.
Also none among us has seen God.
(... We have thought often
The flaws of sun in the late and driving weather
pointed to one tree but it was not so.)
As for the nights I warn you the nights are dangerous:
The wind changes at night and the dreams come.

It is very cold,
                there are strange stars near Arcturus,
Voices are crying an unknown name in the sky
—Archibald Macleish

About the author

Sandy McCulloch is a generalist. He has been a college lecturer in zoology and a psychologist. He built and operated a country inn on thirty-five acres of redwood forest near Mendocino, California. And in later years he has traveled to twenty-five countries on four continents and published seven books of short stories.

He made his grand opera debut in 1954 with the San Francisco Opera Company's production of *Aida*.

Generalists do not become famous, but they have more fun.

CPSIA information can be obtained at www.ICGtesting.com
Printed in the USA
BVOW032052190513

321062BV00006B/89/P